ANIMAL SAFARI

Warthogs

by Megan Borgert-Spaniol

BELLWETHER MEDIA • MINNEAPOLIS, MN

Note to Librarians, Teachers, and Parents:

Blastoff! Readers are carefully developed by literacy experts and combine standards-based content with developmentally appropriate text.

Level 1 provides the most support through repetition of high-frequency words, light text, predictable sentence patterns, and strong visual support.

Level 2 offers early readers a bit more challenge through varied simple sentences, increased text load, and less repetition of high-frequency words.

Level 3 advances early-fluent readers toward fluency through increased text and concept load, less reliance on visuals, longer sentences, and more literary language.

Level 4 builds reading stamina by providing more text per page, increased use of punctuation, greater variation in sentence patterns, and increasingly challenging vocabulary.

Level 5 encourages children to move from "learning to read" to "reading to learn" by providing even more text, varied writing styles, and less familiar topics.

Whichever book is right for your reader, Blastoff! Readers are the perfect books to build confidence and encourage a love of reading that will last a lifetime!

This edition first published in 2013 by Bellwether Media, Inc.

No part of this publication may be reproduced in whole or in part without written permission of the publisher. For information regarding permission, write to Bellwether Media, Inc., Attention: Permissions Department, 5357 Penn Avenue South, Minneapolis, MN 55419.

Library of Congress Cataloging-in-Publication Data
Borgert-Spaniol, Megan, 1989-
  Warthogs / by Megan Borgert-Spaniol.
    p. cm. – (Blastoff! readers: animal safari)
  Includes bibliographical references and index.
  Summary: "Developed by literacy experts for students in kindergarten through grade three, this book introduces warthogs to young readers through leveled text and related photos"–Provided by publisher.
  ISBN 978-1-60014-770-8 (hardcover : alk. paper)
  1. Warthog–Juvenile literature. I. Title.
  QL737.U58B67 2013
  599.63'3–dc23   2011053025

Printed in the United States of America, North Mankato, MN.

Contents

What Are Warthogs?

Warthogs are **wild** pigs. They have long **snouts** and strong **tusks**.

tusk

They also have
bumps on the sides
of their heads.
The bumps are
called warts.

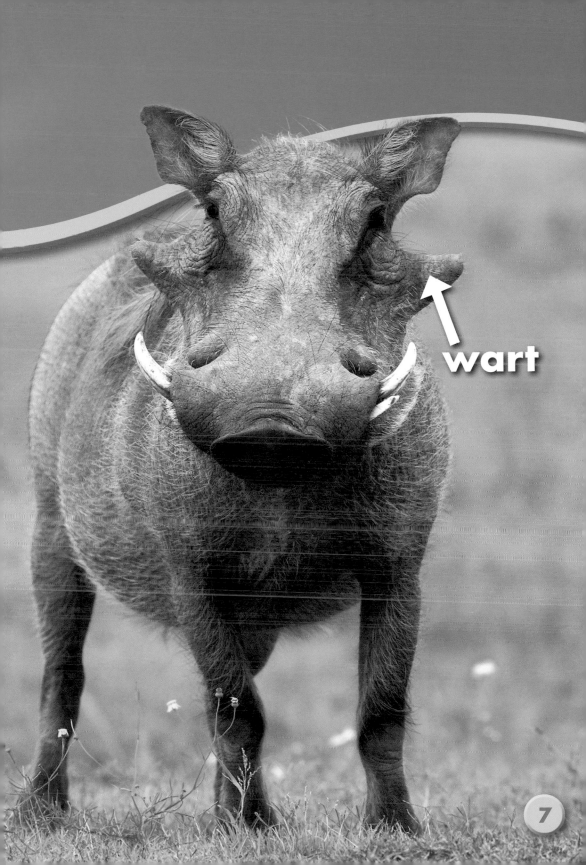

wart

Grazing and Digging

Warthogs **graze** on grasses in **savannahs**. They also eat berries, bark, and roots.

Warthogs dig up roots with their snouts. They kneel on their front legs as they dig.

Fighting

Male warthogs live alone most of the time. Sometimes they fight over a female.

13

They use their tusks to push each other. Their warts protect them from getting hurt.

Females raise their **piglets** in groups called **sounders**. They watch out for lions and leopards.

Warthogs snort loudly and run when they see these **predators**.

The piglets dash into a **burrow** to hide. Their mother guards the burrow with her tusks. Keep out!

Glossary

burrow—a hole or tunnel in the ground; warthogs often use burrows built by other animals.

graze—to feed on plants and grasses

piglets—young warthogs

predators—animals that hunt other animals for food

savannahs—grasslands with very few trees

snouts—the jaws and noses of some animals

sounders—groups of female warthogs and their young

tusks—large, long teeth that stick out of the mouths of some animals

wild—living in nature

To Learn More

AT THE LIBRARY

Napoli, Donna Jo. *Mogo, the Third Warthog.* New York, N.Y.: Hyperion Books for Children, 2008.

Roberts, Patsy Smith. *Willis the Warthog.* Saint Simons Island, Ga.: Savuti Muti Publishing, 2005.

Walden, Katherine. *Warthogs.* New York, N.Y.: PowerKids Press, 2009.

ON THE WEB

Learning more about warthogs is as easy as 1, 2, 3.

1. Go to www.factsurfer.com.

2. Enter "warthogs" into the search box.

3. Click the "Surf" button and you will see a list of related Web sites.

With factsurfer.com, finding more information is just a click away.

Index